THE LITTLE BOOK OF
ELVIS

Compiled by
TREVOR BAKER

CARLTON
BOOKS

Published by Carlton Books Limited 2002

20 Mortimer Street

London W1T 3JW

ISBN 1 84222 880 3

Printed in Singapore

INTRODUCTION

IT'S 25 years since Elvis Presley died. And yet, despite that sad anniversary, the king has never been bigger. If anyone needed proof of his continuing popularity it came with this year's release of 'A Little Less Conversation', his record-breaking eighteenth UK number one.

Ironically, by breaking the Beatles' record for the greatest number of chart-toppers, Elvis ensured that conversations about him would continue forever. Or at least while there are still people listening to Rock 'n' Roll.

Ever since he first stepped up on stage the kid from Tupolo, Mississippi has inspired controversy, love, awe and respect in equal amounts.

In this collection you'll find comments from people who got it and people who didn't, people who knew him as a friend and people who loved him from afar. And, of course, plenty of the dry humour of the king himself. 'A Little Less Conversation?' There's no chance of that.

★ ★ ★ ★ ★ ★ ★ ★ ★ ★ ★ ★ ★ ★

★

❝When I first heard Elvis' voice I just knew that I wasn't going to work for anybody and nobody was going to be my boss. Hearing him for the first time was like busting out of jail.❞

Bob Dylan

★ ★ ★ ★ ★ ★ ★ ★ ★ ★ ★ ★ ★

❝I know that the Lord can give, and the Lord can take away. I might be herding sheep next year.❞

Elvis, *1956*

★ ★ ★ ★ ★ ★ ★ ★ ★ ★ ★ ★ ★ ★ ★

❝I've heard it said that the lurchin', urchin, Elvis the Pelvis, hasn't any kind of singing voice, and I was anxious to hear if there was anything in the rumour. Frankly after 16 of his Rock 'n' Roll ballads, delivered with a ferocious intensity and manoeuvres known in the burlesque business as "all-out grinds and bumps", I still have no way of knowing. I just didn't hear one note or one word he sang. 15,000 screaming youngsters for one and a half hours just wouldn't let me.❞

Hugh Thomson, *Toronto Daily Star, 1958*

‘The first time that I appeared on stage, it scared me to death. I really didn't know what all the yelling was about. I didn't realize that my body was moving. It's a natural thing to me. So to the manager backstage I said, "What'd I do? What'd I do?" And he said, "Whatever it is, go back and do it again."’

Elvis, *1972*

❝I'm still bewildered. Last night's contortionist exhibition at the auditorium was the closest to the jungle I'll ever get.❞

Helen Parmeller, *Ottawa Journal, 1957*

"Man, I was tame compared to what they do now. Are you kidding? I didn't do anything but just jiggle."

Elvis, *1972*

❝Some people tap their feet, some people snap their fingers, and some people sway back and forth. I just sorta do 'em all together, I guess.❞

Elvis, *speaking in 1956, doesn't understand what all the fuss is about.*

★ ★ ★ ★ ★ ★ ★ ★ ★ ★ ★ ★ ★ ★

‘My voice alone is just an ordinary voice. What people come to see is how I use it. If I stand still while I'm singing, I'm dead! ’

Elvis

"You have to put on a show for people in order to draw a crowd. If I just stood out there and sang and didn't move a muscle, then people would say, "My goodness, I can stay home and listen to his records" – you have to give them a show."

Elvis

'Anything that don't frighten
the children is in good taste, far as
I'm concerned. '

Elvis

“She asked me if I could be there by three. I was there by the time she hung up the phone.”

Elvis *recalls being asked by Sun Records boss Sam Phillips' assistant Marion Keisker to come in for an audition.*

Marion Keisker: 'What kind of
singer are you?'
Elvis: 'I sing all kinds.'
Marion Keisker: 'Who do you sound like?'
Elvis: 'I don't sound like nobody.'

The first conversation between **Elvis** *and*
Marion Keisker *of Sun Records.*

❝Rock 'n' Roll is the most brutal, ugly, degenerate, vicious form of expression – lewd, sly, in plain fact, dirty – a rancid-smelling aphrodisiac and the martial music of every side-burned delinquent on the face of the earth.❞

Frank Sinatra *is not impressed with his new rival in 1956.*

I'm just a singer, but Elvis was the embodiment of the whole American culture. Life just wouldn't have been the same without him.

Frank Sinatra, *1977*

There have been many accolades uttered about Elvis' talent and performances through the years, all of which I agree with wholeheartedly. I shall miss him dearly as a friend. He was a warm, considerate and generous man.

Frank Sinatra, *1977*

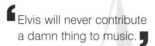

'Elvis will never contribute a damn thing to music.'

Bing Crosby, *1956*

‘The things Elvis has done during his career and the things he has contributed and created are really something very important to the music business. ,

Bing Crosby, *1973*

Elvis helped to kill off the influence of me and my contemporaries, but I respect him for that. Because music always has to progress, and no-one could have opened the door to the future like he did.

Bing Crosby, *1973*

> When he started, he couldn't spell Tennessee. Now he owns it.

Bob Hope

'Mr. Presley has no discernible singing ability. His specialty is rhythm songs which he renders in an undistinguished whine; his phrasing, if it can be called that, consists of the stereotyped variations that go with a beginner's aria in a bathtub. For the ear he is an unutterable bore.'

Jack Gould, *New York Times, 1956*

It isn't enough to say that Elvis is kind to his parents, sends money home, and is the same unspoiled kid he was before all the commotion began. That still isn't a free ticket to behave like a sex maniac in public.

Eddie Condon, *Cosmopolitan, December 1956*

'People who read sex into my music have dirty minds.'

Elvis

Ed Sullivan, *1956*

'I wanted to say to Elvis Presley and the country that this is a real decent, fine boy. '

Ed Sullivan *during Elvis' third appearance on his show. January 6, 1957.*

I watch my audience and listen to them and I know that we're all getting somethin' out of our system, none of us knows what it is – the important thing is we're getting rid of it and nobody's getting hurt.

Elvis

★ ★ ★ ★ ★ ★ ★ ★ ★ ★ ★ ★ ★ ★

I don't like to be called Elvis the Pelvis – it's one of the most childish expressions I've ever heard coming from an adult, but if they want to call me that, there's nothing I can do about it, so I just have to accept it.

Elvis

"When Rock 'n' Roll dies out another type of emotional music is going to take its place. Then I can sit on my back porch at Graceland and remember the good ol' days."

Elvis

'Rock 'n' Roll music – I don't think it'll ever die completely out because they're gonna have to get something mighty good to take its place. '

Elvis

"If they want my boy to sing, they are going to have to pay for it like anyone else."

*The response from **Colonel Tom Parker** to the army's offer of a post in Special Services for the drafted Elvis.*

"I never hated anything so much in my life as I have the army. It's an excellent experience. It lets you find out how other people think and live."

Elvis

'I wouldn't call girls a hobby – it's a pastime.'

Elvis

> *Any man who says he ain't interested is a liar. Any woman who says that, she's probably lyin' too.*

Elvis *on pornography.*

Elvis never was a Casanova type, or libertine. He was more like a pleasant high school date.

Natalie Wood *actress*

Guys, I've just met the prettiest girl I've ever seen, her name is Priscilla. Some day I'll probably marry her.

Elvis *to his friends after coming back from Germany where he met his future wife.*

★ ★ ★ ★ ★ ★ ★ ★ ★ ★ ★ ★ ★ ★

❝The most beautiful thing in the world to me is a baby lookin' as pretty as her mamma.❞

Elvis

⭐

❝Elvis was a man who brought happiness through himself and his music to millions of people around the world. He felt the most important thing he could do was to inspire people. He didn't mean it in a conceited way. . .in fact, he felt it was more of an obligation than anything.❞

Priscilla Presley

⭐ ⭐ ⭐ ⭐ ⭐ ⭐ ⭐ ⭐ ⭐ ⭐ ⭐ ⭐

'A lot of people have accused Elvis of stealing the black man's music, when in fact, almost every black solo entertainer copied his stage mannerisms from Elvis.'

Jackie Wilson

★ ★ ★ ★ ★ ★ ★ ★ ★ ★ ★ ★ ★ ★

> If you hate another human being because of their race, you're hating part of yourself.

Elvis

'He was an integrator. Elvis was a blessing. They wouldn't let black music through. He opened the door for black music. '

Little Richard

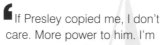

❝If Presley copied me, I don't care. More power to him. I'm not starving.**❞**

Bo Diddley

❝Elvis is the greatest cultural force in the twentieth century. He introduced the beat to everything; music, language, clothes, it's a whole new social revolution – the sixties comes from it.❞

Leonard Bernstein

' Elvis had an influence on everybody with his musical approach. He broke the ice for all of us. '

Al Green

There have been a lotta tough guys. There have been pretenders. And there have been contenders. But there is only one king.

Bruce Springsteen

"He was the firstest with the mostest."

Roy Orbison

Before Elvis, there was nothing.

John Lennon

When you let your head get too big it'll break your neck.

Elvis

There is something magical about watching a man who has lost himself find his way back home. . .He sang with the kind of power people no longer expect from Rock 'n' Roll singers.

A review by **John Landau** *of Elvis' 1968 TV Special.*

'It was the finest music of his life. If ever there was music that bleeds, this was it.'

Rock critic **Greil Marcus** *on the 1968 TV Special.*

★

There are several unbelievable things about Elvis, but the most incredible is his staying power in a world where meteoric careers fade like shooting stars.

Newsweek, *August 11, 1969*

‘You have no idea how great he is, really you don't. You have no comprehension - it's absolutely impossible. I can't tell you why he's so great, but he is. He's sensational.’

Phil Spector

The image is one thing and the human being is another. . .It's very hard to live up to an image.

Elvis, *1972*

"You Memphis politicians had better watch out if Elvis Presley ever decides to enter politics."

George Bush

'You know, Bush is always comparing me to Elvis in sort of unflattering ways. I don't think Bush would have liked Elvis very much, and that's just another thing that's wrong with him.'

Bill Clinton

❝It's always been my dream to come to Madison Square Garden and be the warm-up act for Elvis.❞

Senator Al Gore *is nominated as a candidate to be Vice President, just before Bill Clinton accepts the Democratic Party's nomination for President.*

❝ He was ahead of his time because
he had such deep feelings. He had
the privilege of deep feelings because
he was deeply loved by his mother,
Gladys. He was able to appreciate
profound beauty in sounds. And he
started a musical revolution. They say
all revolutions start from love. ❞

Ousted dictator's wife **Imelda Marcos**
knows all about revolutions.

'I love his music because he was my generation. But then again, Elvis is everyone's generation, and he always will be.'

Margaret Thatcher

❝I'm sitting in the drive-through and I've got my three girls in the back and this station comes on and it's playing "Jailhouse Rock", the original version, and my girls are jumping up and down, going nuts. I'm looking around at them and they've heard Dad's music all the time and I don't see that out of them.❞

*Country singer **Garth Brooks**'*
children have good taste.

'I remember Elvis as a young man hanging around the Sun studios. Even then, I knew this kid had a tremendous talent. He was a dynamic young boy. His phraseology, his way of looking at a song, was as unique as Sinatra's. I was a tremendous fan, and had Elvis lived, there would have been no end to his inventiveness. '

B.B. King

❝I've heard musicians say, "Man, I don't care about Elvis Presley – it don't shake me up to play on his sessions". And then they get on the session and they just go to pieces; just completely go to pieces when he walks in the room. And then after he leaves, they'll say, "Now I see why he's Elvis Presley, man I ain't never been around a guy like that."❞

Felton Jarvis *Elvis' record producer, 1973*

There's no way to describe the excitement of being on stage with Elvis Presley. The joy of seeing him, working with him. . .I've always thought that was one of his secrets of success, that he looked different to anyone I've ever seen in my life. He had a period in his life from the mid-sixties to the mid-seventies when his was the best looking face I've ever looked into. He was beautiful!

Gordon Stoker *backing singer for Elvis in the 1950's & 1960's.*

'Elvis was a rebel, but he was a rebel that had love in his face.'

Jerry Schilling *friend of Elvis*

'Elvis Presley's talent brightened millions of lives. He widened the horizons of *my* world certainly. . .Elvis Presley more than made me feel good, he enriched my life and made it better.'

Stephen King

‟Elvis had the looks on me. The girls were going for him for more reasons than music. Elvis was hittin' 'em with sideburns, flashy clothes and no ring on that finger. I had three kids. There was no way of keeping Elvis from being the man in that music.„

Carl Perkins

' His music was the only thing
exclusively ours. His wasn't my mom
and dad's music. His voice was a total
miracle in the music business. '

Carl Wilson *The Beach Boys*

★ ★ ★ ★ ★ ★ ★ ★ ★ ★ ★ ★ ★ ★

I don't know anything about music.
In my line you don't have to.

Elvis

"I don't want to read about some of these actresses who are around today. They sound like my niece in Scarsdale. I love my niece in Scarsdale, but I won't buy tickets to see her act."

Elvis

★ ★ ★ ★ ★ ★ ★ ★ ★ ★ ★ ★ ★ ★ ★

❝ If life was fair, Elvis would be
alive and the Elvis impersonators
would be dead. **❞**

Talk show host **Johnny Carson** *gets brutal.*

'Gossip is small words from small minds.'

Elvis

★ ★ ★ ★ ★ ★ ★ ★ ★ ★ ★ ★ ★

❝I don't wanna put anybody's job down, reporters have a job to do and they have to write stuff, and if they don't know anything they just make it up.❞

Elvis

❝I got sick one night – a temperature of 102 and they wouldn't let me perform. From three different sources I heard I was 'strung out' on heroin, I swear to God, people spreading rumours, all across this town they said I was 'strung out'. . .If I find the individual who has said that about me, I'm gonna break your god-damn neck you son of a bitch. It is dangerous, it is damaging to myself, to my little daughter, to my father, to my friends and to my fans.**❞**

Elvis

'Truth is like the sun. You can shut it out for a time, but it ain't goin' away.'

Elvis

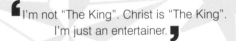

'I'm not "The King". Christ is "The King".
I'm just an entertainer.'

Elvis

❝I don't want to miss out on heaven
because of a technicality.**❞**

*The response from **Elvis** when asked why he wore a
Christian cross, A Star of David and a Hebrew Chi.*

> **'**I owe Elvis my career, and the entire music business owes him its lifeline.**'**

Cliff Richard

‘ Elvis is my religion. If it was not for him, I'd be selling encyclopedias. ’

Bruce Springsteen

> I doubt very much if the Beatles would have happened if it was not for Elvis. God bless you Elvis.

Paul McCartney

'Without Elvis, none of us could have made it.'

Buddy Holly

❝Elvis was God-given, there's no other explanation. A Messiah comes around every few thousand years, and Elvis was it this time.❞

Little Richard

❝The first time I met him I was blown away, I just looked at him and said, "damn, son, you about the best looking thing I ever did see, kinda wish I was a girl right now Elvis."❞

Jerry Reed *country singer*

★ ★ ★ ★ ★ ★ ★ ★ ★ ★ ★ ★ ★ ★

❝I think Elvis is the sexiest man to ever walk the earth. I love him.**❞**

Britney Spears

When I first heard Elvis perform "Bridge Over Troubled Water" it was unbelievable and I thought to myself, "how the hell can I compete with that?"

Paul Simon *writer of* 'Bridge Over Troubled Water'

‘The highlight of my career?
That's easy, Elvis recording one
of my songs. ’

Bob Dylan

‟I had always wanted to be like Elvis, to be a Rock 'n' Roll star, but I couldn't sing so I joined a mod band instead.„

Roger Daltry *The Who*

❝I had a TV show in Odessa, Texas, and we played mainly country music. But after Presley came through town for a show in late 1954 I began to notice the rhythm music. I hope that nobody will ever forget how he influenced us all – he isn't just a historical phenomenon, but rather something very lasting.❞

Roy Orbison

"It was just incredible. In Vegas, I was kidding him. He introduced me and said "Campbell, I understand you're doing a imitation of me, I just want you to know it will always be an imitation", and I said "I'm not going to do it no more, I gotta gain some weight first." He laughed, and the audience went "oooh, hey, booo." I said "can't you take a joke?", Elvis could take it, but the audience just got on my ass."

Glen Campbell *singer*

Once Elvis tried unsuccessfully to convince a group of people outside a Memphis disco that he really was Elvis Presley. Because no one expected Elvis Presley to be out in public.

Charlie Hodge *Elvis aide*

'Elvis showed up about 3 am shopping for cars. He brought 13 Cadillacs in an hour and a half. The bill came to $168,000. They were Christmas presents for his staff.'

*Memphis Cadillac dealer **Pat Gilmore** makes the deal of a lifetime in 1975.*

Elvis was so generous you had to be careful around him. If you said you liked something he'd turn around and give it to you.

Glen D. Hardin *pianist*

'With all the controversy about Elvis' drug-taking and his physical condition toward the end of his life, people often forget what a tank he was. Nobody did what Elvis did in Las Vegas. four weeks, seven days a week, two, sometimes three shows a night. An awesome schedule. But he did it. Those of us who were there now understand that the man was working himself to death.'

Lamar Fike *friend of Elvis*

‘Sometimes when I walk into a room at home and see all the gold records hanging on the walls, I think they must belong to another person, not me, I just can't believe that it's true.’

Elvis

 I wouldn't call any art bad, though there's a lot of it I don't get. I like realism, though. I can admire a good house paintin' job.

Elvis

❝In public, I like real conservative clothes, something that's not too flashy, but onstage, I like them as flashy as you can get them.❞

Elvis

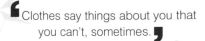

‘Clothes say things about you that
you can't, sometimes. ’

Elvis

'When you're a celebrity, people treat you nicer. The bad part is, they also tell you what they think you want to hear, which ain't always the truth.'

Elvis

The thing I like about success is to know that you've got so many friends, a lot of real close friends that I've made since I've been in the business.

Elvis

> **'**Dogs love you no matter how much you do or don't have. You can count on them more than you can count on most people – they don't leave you like some people do.**'**

Elvis

'I've had a pretty good lesson in human nature, it's more important to try to surround yourself with people who can give you a little happiness, because you can only pass through this life once, Jack – you don't come back for an encore. '

Elvis, *from an article in* Esquire *magazine.*

I didn't know what I wanted to do as a kid. But I used to pray to God that I'd amount to something some day. I never dreamed that something like this would happen.

Elvis

★ ★ ★ ★ ★ ★ ★ ★ ★ ★ ★ ★ ★ ★ ★ ★ ★

'A Presley picture is the only sure thing in Hollywood.'

Hal Wallis *producer of nine of Elvis' films*

'The only thing worse than watchin' a bad movie is bein' in one.'

Elvis

❝I still believe that no matter who they are, whether you be Axl Rose or whoever, the posing came from Elvis. All we did was take it and make it different in little bits, but in the end it was he who gave us all the poses and the reason to pose.❞

Cliff Richard

★ ★ ★ ★ ★ ★ ★ ★ ★ ★ ★ ★ ★ ★ ★

❝Man, he cared about how he looked, he really did. And I don't know how in the hell he thought he could look bad, but he did. He thought his neck was too long. Honestly, he thought his neck was too long. And he looked and he said, "I've never seen anybody with hands this ugly."❞

Sam Phillips *Sun Records impresario*

'Every morning when I woke up and looked out the window, there were at least two hundred kids lined up on the sidewalk outside. Some of them would stay there all day long, just trying to get a glimpse of him. And when he would go out, he was very sweet to them. A lot of people I know would get angry, or impatient, but Elvis is very sweet to the kids, very nice to them. He always spends as much time with them as he can.'

Natalie Wood

There was something just bordering on rudeness about Elvis. He never actually did anything rude, but he always seemed as if he was just going to. On a scale of one to ten, I would rate him eleven.

Sammy Davis Jr.

'At 9.15 Elvis appeared, materialized, in a white suit of lights, shining with golden appliqués, the shirt front slashed to show his chest. Around his shoulders was a cape lined in a cloth of gold, its collar faced with scarlet. It was anything you wanted to call it, gaudy, vulgar, magnificent.'

New York Times

'I've never gotten over what they call stagefright. I go through it every show. I'm pretty concerned, I'm pretty much thinking about the show. I never get completely comfortable with it, and I don't let the people around me get comfortable with it, in that I remind them that it's a new crowd out there, it's a new audience, and they haven't seen us before. So it's got to be like the first time we go on. '

Elvis, *1972*

"Even back then, when people would laugh at his sideburns and his pink coat and call him "cissy" – he had a pretty hard road to go. In some areas motorcycle gangs would come to the shows. They would come to get Elvis, but he never worried about it. He went right out and did his thing and before the show was over, they were standing in line to get his autograph too."

Carl Perkins

'When we first came to town, these guys like Dean Martin and Frank Sinatra and all these people wanted to come over and hang around with us at night simply because we had all the women, all the chicks. We don't want to meet those people. They don't really like us. We don't really admire or like them. The only person that we wanted to meet in the United States of America was Elvis Presley. We can't tell you what a thrill that was last night.'

John Lennon

In the fifties, Elvis came to one of my shows in Memphis, at the city auditorium. You could have lit a cigarette from him – that's how hot he was. The money from the show went for Little League baseball uniforms and stuff for the children of Memphis, black, white and otherwise. Elvis was into that. They call him 'The King', and I agree.

B.B. King

❛Elvis was the equivalent of Johnny Rotten. When he was playing live in his early days, he would go out on stage with these Country & Western singers and spit his gum out in the crowd. That's why I like to think of him in the years before he went into the army – when he was the Sex Pistols and the Ramones all rolled into one.❜

Joe Perry *Aerosmith*

❝When I think of Graceland, I think of that enormous sofa. Let's just say he was a creature-comfort pioneer. He had a custom made sofa, this "El Grande" supersofa. The guy knew how to live.❞

Bridget Fonda

'When I first met Elvis he had a million dollars worth of talent. Now he has a million dollars.'

By then **Colonel Tom Parker** *had a million dollars too.*

'Rock 'n' Roll is a music. Why should a music contribute to juvenile delinquency? If people are gonna be delinquents they're gonna be delinquents if they hear Mother Goose rhymes. Rock 'n' Roll does not contribute to juvenile delinquency at all.'

Elvis, *1956*

❛I never realized anything like this was possible, that I'd ever be in Hawaii, or Las Vegas, or Hollywood. It's quite a change to jump into this stuff. If you're not careful, you'll crack up.❜

Elvis, *1956*

> I've seen a UFO, never any ghosts. But I believe in an afterlife, so it's possible. When I'm home I can feel my mama's presence.

Elvis

‘Elvis Presley's death deprives our country of a part of itself. He was unique, irreplaceable. He burst upon the scene with an impact that was unprecedented and will probably never be equalled. His music and his personality permanently changed the face of American popular culture. And he was a symbol to people the world over of the vitality, rebelliousness and good humour of this country.’

The official statement from **President Jimmy Carter** *following Elvis' death in 1977.*

'My partner and I had been called to a domestic dispute. When we got there, this couple was just about to kill each other. We pulled them apart. . .Just then, it came over our walkie-talkie unit that Elvis had died. The woman started crying and the man went limp and they went to watching TV and talking about Elvis. It was real strange. We left and didn't hear anything more from them that night.'

Deputy Sheriff Curt Willis *Shelby County, Tennessee, remembers the night Elvis died.*

'I didn't talk to anyone for a week after Elvis died.'

Bob Dylan

'I've lost a very dear friend and the world has lost a great entertainer.'

Ann Margret *actress*

★ ★ ★ ★ ★ ★ ★ ★ ★ ★ ★ ★ ★ ★

"I wasn't just a fan, I was his brother. He said I was good and I said he was good; we never argued about that. Elvis was a hard worker, dedicated, and God loved him. Last time I saw him was at Graceland. We sang "Old Blind Barnabus" together, a gospel song. I love him and hope to see him in heaven. There'll never be another like that soul brother."

James Brown

The name and face of Elvis is one of the most recognizable on Planet Earth. In fact, I am predicting here that, one day, this planet will be renamed Planet Elvis. It will take about 150 to 200 years for this to happen.

Bill Slater *Elvis fansite editor*

> "Talent is bein' able to sell what you're feeling."

Elvis

> ❝ Do you know how hard it is to fake your own death? Only one man has pulled it off: Elvis. ❞

Agent Mulder *to* **Agent Scully** *in the* X-Files.

' I wanted a bicycle. **,**

Elvis *recalls his reaction to being given an*
acoustic guitar for his eleventh birthday.